UNPLUGGED ACTIVITIES FOR FUTURE CODERS

BUILD YOUR DEBUGGING SKILLS

Kathy Furgang and Christopher Harris

Illustrations by Joel Gennari

Enslow Publishing
101 W. 23rd Street
Suite 240
New York, NY 10011
USA

enslow.com

Published in 2020 by Enslow Publishing, LLC
101 W. 23rd Street, Suite 240, New York, NY 10011

Library of Congress Cataloging-in-Publication Data

Names: Furgang, Kathy, author. | Harris, Christopher, author. |
Gennari, Joel, illustrator.
Title: Build your debugging skills / Kathy Furgang and Christopher Harris ;
illustrations by Joel Gennari.
Description: New York : Enslow Publishing, 2020. | Series: Unplugged
activities for future coders | Audience: Grades: 5 to 8. | Includes
bibliographical references and index.
Identifiers: LCCN 2019000157| ISBN 9781978510685 (library bound) | ISBN
9781978510678 (pbk.)
Subjects: LCSH: Debugging in computer science—Juvenile literature. |
Debugging in computer science—Study and teaching—Activity programs.
Classification: LCC QA76.9.D43 F87 2020 | DDC 004.2/4—dc23
LC record available at https://lccn.loc.gov/2019000157

Printed in the United States of America

To Our Readers: We have done our best to make sure all website addresses in this book were active and appropriate when we went to press. However, the author and the publisher have no control over and assume no liability for the material available on those websites or on any websites they may link to. Any comments or suggestions can be sent by email to customerservice@enslow.com.

Image Credits: Character illustrations by Joel Gennari, other art by Christine Pekatowski.

CONTENTS

INTRODUCTION

If you are writing code and it doesn't work the first time, don't despair. In the real world of computer programming, this is an everyday occurrence. When code doesn't work, look at it as an opportunity to practice your debugging skills. "Debugging" is the coding term for finding and fixing errors. There is both an art and a science to debugging code.

Debugging consists of two separate actions: finding and fixing. While your programs might be quite short as you start out, real programs can have thousands or even millions of lines of code.

Imagine just one error among millions of lines of code. There must be a trick to finding it, right? Not always. The practice of stepping through each line of code is one of the best skills you can develop as a programmer. Not only is it helpful for finding and fixing bugs, it also helps you follow through the logic of your code to make sure you are on the right path.

When you trace the code you have written, your brain becomes the computer. You literally work through each line of code and check it. For example, codes must use the correct punctuation for the computer language you are using. If a computer language sets statements apart using parentheses () or brackets {}, then the correct opening and closing bracket must be in exactly the right place.

You can think of decoding as proofreading an essay for typos or punctuation errors. If something is wrong with the wording, the meaning might change. The sentence might not make any sense at all. Or, imagine you wrote some lines of music. If every note is not correct, the sound of the music will change. Or it may just sound awful. Similarly, if you run a computer program with errors in the code, the program will not work correctly. In many cases, the program will not run at all.

Thinking like a computer debugger takes skill. But it doesn't always take computer coding skills. The skills needed most for debugging are patience, determination, and logic. If you have the patience to read through lines of code looking for that one thing that doesn't quite make sense, then you might make a great debugger.

The activities in this book do not require a computer because they are meant to develop your thinking skills. Many can be done with just pencil and paper. You will get the chance to create instructions, make an error, and challenge a friend to find the problem.

The twelve activities increase with difficulty and complexity. Start out slow and work your way through to the activities that are longer and require more thought.

Each activity will list the number of players required and a suggestion for the amount of time you might need to devote to it. You will then be guided through your "mission" with step-by-step instructions and a way to review what you've learned. The reviews are meant to make you think about how the activities apply to real-world coding and debugging situations.

The activities can even be done more than once. The directions are open enough so that you can create different puzzles or codes and use them with different friends. Once you have mastered some of the activities in the book, you might feel more confident to conquer debugging problems in real lines of code.

DEBUG!

 *10–15 minutes*

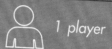 *1 player*

YOUR MISSION

Debugging may sound like a foreign term, but it's really simple: If something doesn't work, it needs to be fixed. If you've ever checked your work on a math problem and changed your answer, congratulations— you're a debugger! Finding errors in code can be tricky, so debuggers have to be quick-thinking problem solvers.

It tends to be a lot easier to find a bug than it is to fix one. For example, 2 – 2 = 4 is a buggy statement. Either the operator is wrong—a minus sign instead of a plus sign—or the answer is wrong and it should be 0. But which is it? Pro debuggers have to look at the code around the problem to figure it out, and you will, too.

Your Gear

- **Pencil**
- **Paper**

LET'S PLAY

How good are you at spotting bugs? Read through the following pseudocode examples and see if you can find all the problems. Think about what the programmer expects the code to do as compared to what is written. If you get stuck, try to follow each command in your head or on paper and make sure everything works.

DRAWING A RECTANGLE USING A ROBOT

1. Print "How long should the rectangle be?"
2. Get <Distance> from user input
3. Drive Robot Forward <Distance>
4. Turn 90 Degrees Right
5. Drop Pen
6. Drive Robot Forward 10/2
7. Turn 90 Degrees Left
8. Drive Robot Forward <Distance>
9. Turn 90 Degrees Right
10. Drive Robot Backward <Distance>/2
11. Pick Up Pen

MOVING BOXES USING A ROBOT

1. Print "How many boxes do you need to move today?"
2. Get <NumBoxes> from user input
3. Repeat 5 times
   a. Drive to Box Pickup
   b. Pick up box
   c. Drive to Box Dropoff
   d. Pick up box
   e. Print "Your boxes are all moved."

GETTING READY TO GO OUTSIDE

1. Check the Weather
2. IF it is Raining THEN Get Umbrella
3. IF it is Snowing THEN Get Winter Boots ELSE Get Rain Boots
4. IF Temperature > 40 degrees THEN Get Warm Coat ELSE Get Light Jacket
5. ELSE Wear Hat

REVIEW YOUR MOVES

• Are some parts of code, such as IF/THEN statements, more likely to contain bugs? Are some less likely to?

• What would happen if your debugging fix created more bugs? Maybe there's an issue somewhere else now!

Code Editors

Programmers often write their code using special programs called an integrated development environment (IDE). The IDE often combines a code editor and two debugging tools that help programmers. The code editor is like a special version of a word processor that has rules for different programming languages. A code editor will help make sure you remember to use the correct punctuation for your language. For languages that set statements apart using parentheses () or brackets {}, a code editor will also make sure that if you open a (you also close it with a) some time later! Using a code editor with these types of features can help prevent simple punctuation bugs. There are free code editors you can download or use online. https://repl.it/ is an online editor and test environment where you can try out many different languages.

THE PROBLEM IS. . .

 *15–20 minutes*

 *2+ players*

YOUR MISSION

Bugs always seem to show up in software. Debuggers have to find these errors and squash them so that programs run as intended. But even once you know *what* the problem is, you still have to figure out what's causing it and how to solve it!

LET'S PLAY

One person in your group is going to have to pretend to be a computer, and the rest of the players will pretend to be debugging pros. The computer will come up with an everyday activity, such as brushing their teeth, and think of something that might stop them from completing the task.

For example: "I was trying to finish my task, but the problem was the tube was almost empty."

The debugging squad needs to figure out both this mystery task and how they might fix it!

For example: "Did you try rolling up the tube from the bottom to let you finish brushing your teeth?"

If the task is guessed correctly, it is the next player's turn to become the computer.

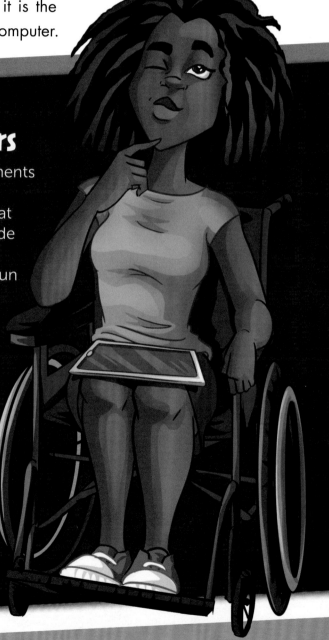

Real-World Debuggers

Integrated development environments (IDEs) help with debugging. Most IDEs have a code-building tool that compiles the code. Compiling code turns it from the programming language into binary that can be run by the computer. Many bugs will be caught during the compiling stage, so using an integrated tool can help you identify a specific line of code that is causing the problem. Finally, an IDE may have a set of actual debugging tools. Debuggers look through the code line by line to see what is going wrong. They let you see each step of code being executed so you can follow the logic of the program to find errors.

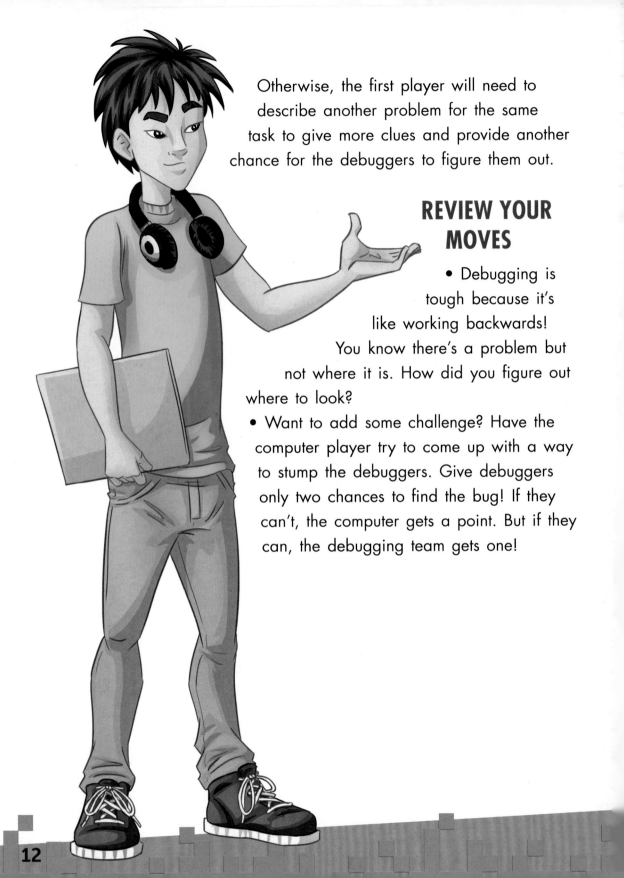

Otherwise, the first player will need to describe another problem for the same task to give more clues and provide another chance for the debuggers to figure them out.

REVIEW YOUR MOVES

- Debugging is tough because it's like working backwards! You know there's a problem but not where it is. How did you figure out where to look?
- Want to add some challenge? Have the computer player try to come up with a way to stump the debuggers. Give debuggers only two chances to find the bug! If they can't, the computer gets a point. But if they can, the debugging team gets one!

OOPS. . .I CAN FIX THAT

 20–30 minutes  3 players

YOUR MISSION

Computers can follow a long list of instructions to complete complex tasks—but only if the instructions include all the necessary steps! A computer can't understand things that it hasn't been programmed to do. Write instructions—with an error!—and challenge someone to find and fix your mistake.

LET'S PLAY

Imagine you must write how-to instructions for an alien from outer space. The alien does not know how to do anything except read English. Choose an everyday activity and write detailed instructions. You might choose an activity such as how to brush your teeth, make a bed, use a cell phone, or play soccer.

Be as detailed as possible with your instructions. Even include when the alien must pick up or put down an item. For example, if you have

never brushed your teeth before, you would need to know when to pick up the toothbrush and the toothpaste, and when to take off the cap. Remember to describe every detail about the task. What do you do with the cap after you have taken it off the toothpaste? When do you open your mouth? What happens next?

Next, add an error to your instructions. It can be tiny and hard to figure out. Or it can be pretty obvious. It depends on how hard you want to make your puzzle.

Give your written instructions to two friends. One is the alien from outer space who follows the instructions exactly. The other is an earthling friend who identifies the error based on the written instructions. Have your earthling friend debug and fix the instructions! Then you follow the corrected instructions yourself!

REVIEW YOUR MOVES

• Try to summarize your activity, error, and fix in one sentence each. For example: I wrote instructions for _____. The problem was, I _____. So someone had to fix it by writing: _____.

• Switch places with your friends and try it again. Each of you should take turns being the alien and the earthling until everyone has done each task.

TRIANGLE MAKERS

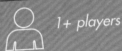 15–20 minutes

1+ players

YOUR MISSION

One way to program instructions for a computer is to set up rules so the computer knows what it can and can't do. These types of rules exist in math, too. Drawing a triangle sounds easy, right? It's just three lines that connect at three corners. But in order to connect, the sides have to be the right length. Let's make triangles!

Your Gear

- **Ruler**
- **Scissors**
- **Pencil**
- **Paper**

LET'S PLAY

Triangles follow a simple rule: the sum of the length of any two sides of a triangle must be greater than the length of the third side. An inequality for this rule would look like this if the three sides of a triangle are named A, B, and C:

A + B > C
B + C > A
A + C > B

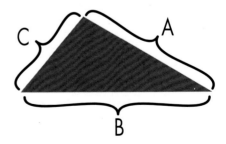

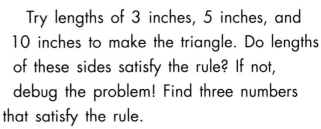

Try lengths of 3 inches, 5 inches, and 10 inches to make the triangle. Do lengths of these sides satisfy the rule? If not, debug the problem! Find three numbers that satisfy the rule.

Once you find a possible way to make a triangle, use the numbers for A, B, and C as inches and use a ruler to draw and cut out a strip of paper that is each length.

Now try to make a right triangle out of the strips. Can you do it? How can you change the length of just one strip to make the problem work?

REVIEW YOUR MOVES

- How many tries did it take you to find three numbers that satisfy the rule?
- Choose the lengths of two sides of a triangle. Challenge a friend to find the length of the third side.

BINARY BONKERS

 15–20 minutes   1+ players

YOUR MISSION

Computers communicate in a language called binary code. All letters and numbers are represented by a combination of 0s and 1s. A long line of binary code can be very difficult to read and discover errors in, but you can get an idea of how it works using a simple chart! You'll decode a binary message, find the error, and rewrite it. Then check your work by rewriting the message.

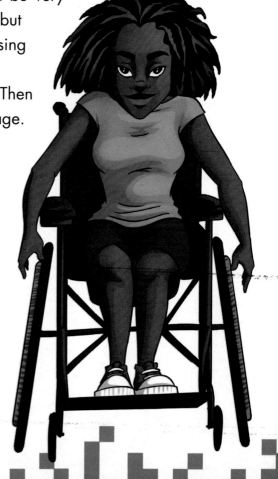

Your Gear

- **Pencil and paper**

LET'S PLAY

The chart that follows gives the binary code that corresponds to each letter of the uppercase alphabet. Use the chart to decode the mixed-up message that follows.

BINARY CHART

A - 01000001	N - 01001110
B - 01000010	O - 01001111
C - 01000011	P - 01010000
D - 01000100	Q - 01010001
E - 01000101	R - 01010010
F - 01000110	S - 01010011
G - 01000111	T - 01010100
H - 01001000	U - 01010101
I - 01001001	V - 01010110
J - 01001010	W - 01010111
K - 01001011	X - 01011000
L - 01001100	Y - 01011001
M - 01001101	Z - 01011010

MIXED-UP MESSAGE

01000110	01001001	01010110	01000100
01000001	01001110	01010000	
01000110	01001111	01011000	

Now that you have decoded the message, does it make sense? Write what it should have said. Then consult the chart to write the binary code for the correct message.

Binary Code

In computer science, binary code is one of the earliest languages to represent data. The system uses 1 and 0 as the only symbols, and the number, combination, and position of the 0s and 1s represents letters and numbers. The 0 or 1 in a binary code are bits. They are the smallest units of notation. A string of bits together is called a byte. In binary code, eight bits together represent a byte. Each letter of the alphabet is expressed as a different byte. The combinations for uppercase letters are different than those for lowercase letters. Mathematical systems such as decimals can also be converted to binary codes, so there are endless ways to represent data with binary code.

REVIEW YOUR MOVES

• Check the way you fixed the message to make sure you copied every byte correctly. If you make your own error when you recopy the message, you did not debug the problem.

• Write your own binary message. Sneak in an error and have a friend debug it!

DEBUG A TOWER

 10–15 minutes

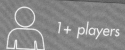 1+ players

YOUR MISSION

For programmers who are debugging a problem, they might find that the error was something as small as one character missing in a line of code. But it could be a much bigger issue! The programmer might have to start over from the beginning and approach the problem from an entirely new angle.

Your Gear

- **Wooden popsicle sticks**
- **Straws**
- **Rubber bands**
- **Masking tape**
- **Tennis ball**

LET'S PLAY

Start off by gathering some basic building materials. Using these items—and only these items—try to design and build a tower that you think will support the weight of a tennis ball. If you get stuck, or your tower collapses, try rethinking your approach! This is similar to what a debugger will do to troublesome code. How could you make your popsicle-stick tower sturdier?

After you've made a strong tower, try thinking of a new way of building one! There are countless ways to work any problem out.

REVIEW YOUR MOVES

• Think you're a master builder? Grab a friend and a stopwatch and really push yourself! Set a time limit—for instance, five minutes—and use simple materials to race against your friend. The goal? Make a tower that can support a tennis ball as tall as possible within the time limit.

• How did you overcome the challenges of building a tower? What strategies did you use to get past a major obstacle?

CLOSE UP SHOP!

 10–15 minutes

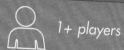 1+ players

YOUR MISSION

Binary code is the most basic code used in computing, but programmers have developed lots of other codes or languages to create websites and applications. One of them is HTML, which stands for hyperlink markup language. It is a language for tagging, or marking, text that appears on websites. Learn how to read basic HTML tags—and how to debug them!

Your Gear

- **Pencil and paper**

LET'S PLAY

HTML uses tags, or a series of symbols, to describe how to display certain elements so that a website is formatted properly. When checking whether there is a mistake in a line of code, programmers will look for things like missing or incorrect tags.

Some punctuation, such as opening and closing brackets, has its own HTML tags. For example, the box on the following page shows the tags for left and right brackets and curly braces.

Left square bracket [	Right square bracket]	Left curly brace {	Right curly brace }
&#91;	&#93;	&#123;	&#125;

Check the codes below to look for errors. The brackets and braces have been replaced with their tags. But something is wrong with the codes. Debug it!

]Here is my favorite website.}
[Do you like it too?{

The code should read:
{Here is my favorite website.}
[Do you like it too?]

REVIEW YOUR MOVES

• Write your own messages with brackets or curly braces. Make an error or two and have a friend debug it.
• Write another message in which you leave one of the brackets out. Have a friend figure out which bracket was left out (bracket or brace), and fix the code to open or close the message.

SKETCHY CHARACTERS

 10–15 minutes

 2+ players

YOUR MISSION

HTML code has lots of different tags to represent elements on a website. Other programming languages use different tags and symbols. Expert programmers learn all kinds of tags by heart so they can spot mistakes in them more quickly.

Your Gear

- **Pencil and paper**

LET'S PLAY

Consult the chart on the following page. Each characteristic is represented by the three- to six-character code that is shown.

Draw a face using the traits listed. Pick two characteristics for hair: one for length and one for style. Then choose a trait for the mouth and eyes.

Hair	Mouth	Eyes
Long *^$	Smiling with teeth showing LRPW	No glasses, eyes open 2934
Short #!(&)	Smiling without teeth showing EBKS	No glasses, eyes closed 9012
Curly J%3@^	Sticking tongue out QTONM	Eyeglasses 883012
Straight)?/=#	Making a fish face CBWKL	Sunglasses 199203

Show your drawing to a friend. Have him or her draw the code to represent your drawing. There should be an underscore between each trait. For example, a sketch that shows a character with long, curly hair, a tongue sticking out, and sunglasses should be coded like this:

*^$_J%3@^_QTONM_199203

Check your friend's work. If there are errors…debug them!

A Big Business

Debugging is an extremely important part of the software industry. Many software development companies spend about half their programming time on debugging. That translates to hundreds of billions of dollars per year. Debugging software that can cut down on debugging time could be a valuable tool. According to a study by the University of Cambridge Judge Business School, reducing debugging time by just 26 percent can save more than $81 billion in the software industry worldwide.

REVIEW YOUR MOVES

• Write a code for a character and include one or more errors. Have a friend try to draw the character, find the error, and fix it.

• Think of other traits and make your own codes and sketches to match the new traits.

MYSTERY MAP

 20-30 minutes

 2 players

YOUR MISSION

Debugging the mistakes in a line of code is kind of like tracing your way through a maze. But like on a map, there are familiar landmarks to help the programmer find the way. In coding, the landmarks will be tags and symbols from the programming language. On a map, the familiar items can be marked in a map key. On a map of the United States, rivers might be blue and capital cities might have a star next to their names. What items would you put on a key to a map of your home?

Your Gear

- **Graph paper**
- **Pencil and paper**
- **Scissors**
- **Colored pencils**

LET'S PLAY

Use graph paper to draw a map of your home or a section of your home. If you want, include details such as hallways, rooms, furniture, counters, or appliances. Color the map to match a map key that identifies items in different colors.

Make a small "game piece" of a person or animal that can be moved through the map, staying mainly within the squares of the graph paper. Cut the game piece out.

Using the boxes of the graph paper as a guide, write simple instructions to move your game piece from one place on the map to another. Sample instructions might read:

- Start at the box in front left corner, in front of the refrigerator.
- Move three spaces to the left.
- Turn right and move eight spaces.
- Move four spaces to enter the living room.
- Turn left and move twelve spaces to the couch.

The set of directions will be your "correct" code. Now write the instructions in a paragraph form and include at least one error.

Give your map, paragraph, and game piece to a friend. Have him or her draw the path on the graph paper to reflect the instructions. This will show where the "bugs" in the code are located.

Have your partner rewrite the paragraph to fix the bugs. Draw the corrected path in a pencil of a different color.

REVIEW YOUR MOVES

• Rewrite and correct the paragraph that gives directions around the map.

• Play the activity off the paper. Write instructions around locations in your home and include some errors for a friend to debug.

LOGIC PUZZLES

 *10–15 minutes*

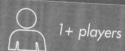 *1+ players*

YOUR MISSION

Test your logic with some puzzles! Logic puzzles are a classic example of deduction in games. Deduction is a type of logic—it means coming to a conclusion based on specific information. It's Sherlock Holmes's favorite tool! Ready to test your problem-solving skills? Logic puzzles are the perfect way to see if you're ready for the big leagues. You'll only get a few clues to figure everything out!

Your Gear

- **Pencil**
- **Paper**
- **Ruler**

LET'S PLAY

To complete a logic puzzle, you must carefully read each clue and figure out what it is stating. Logic puzzles use a grid system to keep track of what the statements mean. If a statement tells you that a combination is false, meaning it is not possible, then mark that space in the grid with an X.

It's always a good idea to find the statements that are true. Once a space is marked with a checkmark for being true, none of the other spaces in that row (across) or column (up and down) can be true. There is only one correct answer! That means you can then mark all of the other spaces in the row and column of the true answer with Xs, because they're definitely false.

Check out the example below before moving on to your own puzzle:

Four friends went into an ice cream shop. Each person ordered a different flavor of ice cream. What kind of ice cream did Callie order? Here are your clues:

1. Brian got ice cream with nuts in it.
2. Alisha likes things mixed into her ice cream.
3. Dominic doesn't like chocolate.

The first statement is a true statement. You know that Brian gets a checkmark for butter pecan because no other flavor has nuts in it. Remember that there can only be one checkmark per row and column—which means you can mark some Xs, too!

	Alisha	Brian	Callie	Dominic
Vanilla		X		
Chocolate		X		
Strawberry		X		
Butter Pecan	X	✔	X	X

From the second statement, you learn that Alisha had either strawberry or butter pecan. No other flavor has bits mixed in. Since you know Brian ordered butter pecan, you now know Alisha must have ordered strawberry! That means you get to mark a check and some more Xs.

	Alisha	Brian	Callie	Dominic
Vanilla	X	X		
Chocolate	X	X		
Strawberry	✔	X	X	X
Butter Pecan	X	✔	X	X

Since Dominic definitely didn't order chocolate ice cream, his only other option is vanilla. Once you mark that, you're left with the answer to the logic puzzle: Callie must have ordered chocolate!

	Alisha	Brian	Callie	Dominic
Vanilla	X	X	X	✔
Chocolate	X	X	✔	X
Strawberry	✔	X	X	X
Butter Pecan	X	✔	X	X

Now that you're a logical master, try a puzzle out for yourself! You can make grids so that other people can give it a try. Figure out how many rows and columns you'll need. Remember to include space for the labels as well as the boxes where the puzzle solvers will put Xs and check marks. Then use the ruler and pencil to draw the grid. Fill in the labels.

REVIEW YOUR MOVES

• Think you're smarter than your parents? Challenge them to a puzzle-off! See who can complete their logic puzzle the fastest.

• Debugging is a lot like filling out a puzzle board—your clues never give up the answer right away.

WHAT'S MY FAVORITE VIDEO GAME?

 20–30 minutes  2+ players

YOUR MISSION

Logic puzzles use the same skills used in debugging. You have to carefully think through the possibilities and check your work to make sure there are no mistakes. Can you follow the clues to find everyone's favorite video game? What clues would you write in your own logic puzzle?

Your Gear

- **Pencil and paper**

LET'S PLAY

Each person on the chart on the following page has a different favorite video game. Copy the chart onto your paper. Read the clues below. If a statement tells you that a combination is false, meaning it is not possible, then mark that space in the grid with an X. Use the clues and the table below to help find out Shari's favorite video game.

CLUES:

- Daria's favorite game is Fever Pitch.
- Play Away is not Shari's or Nick's favorite game.
- Nick's favorite game is not the same as Paolo's or Daria's.
- Attack Mode is not Nick's or Paolo's favorite game.

	Nick	Shari	Paolo	Daria
Fever Pitch				
Play Away				
Sing Song				
Attack Mode				

Once you've solved it, play with a friend! See if your friend can figure out Shari's favorite video game from the clues.

Then fill out the chart again with your own information. Ask friends to tell you their favorite video game. Find four different answers and make a list of clues for your own puzzle. Before having a friend solve the puzzle, check it for bugs. Is every clue correct? Does it lead to the right answers? If not, find the problem and fix it.

REVIEW YOUR MOVES

• Add another friend's favorite video game to the chart. What will you have to do to the clues to add that new friend and game to the chart?

• Would the chart work if two friends had the same favorite video game? Why or why not?

DEBUGGING: EXTERMINATOR LEVEL

 20–30 minutes

 3+ players

YOUR MISSION

Now that you've learned all about debugging and how to use codes like binary code, you're ready to solve an encoded message! Find and fix three types of errors in a binary-coded message.

Your Gear

- **Pencil and paper**

LET'S PLAY

Binary codes for uppercase and lowercase letters can be used to write a message. Use the chart on the following page to decode the binary message below. You will find one underscore between letters in a word.

01011001_01101111_01110101

01100001_01110010_01100101_01100001

01101100_01101001_01111010_01100001_01110010_01100100

01100001_01110100

01100100_01100101_01100010_01110101_01000111_01100111_
01101001_01101110_01100111

BINARY CHART

Uppercase Letters	Lowercase Letters
A - 01000001	a - 01100001
B - 01000010	b - 01100010
C - 01000011	c - 01100011
D - 01000100	d - 01100100
E - 01000101	e - 01100101
F - 01000110	f - 01100110
G - 01000111	g - 01100111
H - 01001000	h - 01101000
I - 01001001	i - 01101001
J - 01001010	j - 01101010
K - 01001011	k - 01101011
L - 01001100	l - 01101100
M - 01001101	m - 01101101
N - 01001110	n - 01101110
O - 01001111	o - 01101111
P - 01010000	p - 01110000
Q - 01010001	q - 01110001
R - 01010010	r - 01110010
S - 01010011	s - 01110011
T - 01010100	t - 01110100
U - 01010101	u - 01110101
V - 01010110	v - 01110110
W - 01010111	w - 01110111
X - 01011000	x - 01111000
Y - 01011001	y - 01111001
Z - 01011010	z - 01111010

What does the message say? There are three different bugs in the message. Debug it! Hint: One problem is a spelling error that makes one of the words incorrect. One is a letter that is in the wrong case. One is an error in spacing—it's either a missing space or a space in the wrong place.

Find all three errors and rewrite the message and binary code correctly.

REVIEW YOUR MOVES

• Make your own message for a friend to decode. Include at least two errors. Give your friend a hint, if necessary, to tell what he or she should keep an eye out for, such as errors in spelling, capitalization, or spacing.

ANSWER KEY

DEBUG! ANSWERS:

DRAWING A RECTANGLE USING A ROBOT BUGS:

- Line 5 (Drop Pen) needs to come before the first drive command.
- In line 6, it needs to use the <Distance> variable, not a set value of 10.
- In line 7, the robot needs to turn right.
- In line 10, the robot needs to drive forward.

MOVING BOXES USING A ROBOT BUGS:

- In line 3, it should repeat using the variable <NumBoxes> not the set number 5.
- In line 3d, it needs to drop off the box, not pick it back up.
- Line 3e needs to become line 4 outside of the repeat statement.

GETTING READY TO GO OUTSIDE BUGS:

- Line 3 means that the algorithm will always say to wear rain boots if the weather is anything other than snow. There should be a second IF to check for rain/rain boots.
- In line 4, the > needs to be a < or the warm coat/light jacket needs to be swapped in THEN/ELSE.
- Line 5 has an ELSE statement, but there isn't an IF/THEN that it connects to.

BINARY BONKERS ANSWERS:

The message says "FIVD ANP FOX." Rewrite as "FIND AND FIX" in binary code:

01000110 01001001 01001110 01000100

01000001 01001110 01000100

01000110 01001001 01011000

CLOSE UP SHOP! ANSWERS:

The right square bracket and left curly brace are in the wrong position. The correct answer should look like:

{Here is my favorite website.}
[Do you like it too?]

WHAT'S MY FAVORITE VIDEO GAME? ANSWERS:

Shari's favorite video game is Attack Mode.

	Nick	Shari	Paolo	Daria
Fever Pitch	X	X	X	✔
Play Away	X	X	✔	X
Sing Song	✔	X	X	X
Attack Mode	X	✔	X	X

DEBUGGING: EXTERMINATOR LEVEL ANSWERS:

Incorrect Message:

You area lizard at debuGging

Correct Message:

You are a wizard at debugging

Correct binary code:

01011001_01101111_01110101

01100001_01110010_01100101

01100001

01110111_01101001_01111010_01100001_01110010_01100100

01100001_01110100

01100100_01100101_01100010_01110101_01100111_01100111_
01101001_01101110_01100111

GLOSSARY

application A kind of software designed to complete specific tasks.

binary Related to two things. The prefix "bi" means "two."

binary code A coding system that uses the digits 0 and 1 to represent other numbers, letters, or characters.

bit The smallest unit of data in a computer code; the 0 or 1 in binary code is a bit.

byte A string of bits in computer code, usually equal to eight bits. Computers nowadays can store many billions of bytes (gigabytes) or even a trillion bytes (a terabyte).

character A symbol—for example, a letter, number, or punctuation mark— that is used for writing or math.

coding The act of writing computer programs using specific programming languages.

data Information in numerical form often used on computers.

debugging A term in coding for finding and fixing errors, or "bugs."

deduction A way of thinking in order to come to a conclusion based on specific information.

inequality A mathematical statement that says two or more values are not equal. It uses the symbol "<" for "less than" or ">" for "greater than."

integrated Describes something that has various parts that are connected.

logic Using reasoning to think about something in an organized way.

notation A way of writing something.

programmer A person who writes (or codes) computer applications or programs.

pseudocode Instructions that are written in language similar to code but understandable by humans.

software Programs that a computer uses.

FURTHER READING

BOOKS

Beedie, Duncan, and Young Rewired State. *Get Coding!: Learn HTML, CSS, and JavaScript and Build a Website, App, and Game.* Somerville, MA: Candlewick Press, 2017.

Loya, Allyssa. *Bugs and Errors with Wreck-It Ralph* (Disney Coding Adventures). Minneapolis, MN: Lerner Publications, 2019.

Lyons, Heather, and Elizabeth Tweedale. *Coding, Bugs and Fixes* (Kids Get Coding). Minneapolis, MN: Lerner Publishing Group, 2017.

Pratt, Jeff. *Getting to Know HTML Code* (Code Power: A Teen Programmer's Guide). New York, NY: Rosen Publishing, 2019.

Wainewright, Max. *How to Code: A Step-by-Step Guide to Computer Coding.* New York, NY: Sterling Children's Books, 2016.

Wood, Kevin. *Get Coding with Debugging* (Computer-Free Coding). New York, NY: Windmill Books, 2018.

WEBSITES

Debugging in Scratch: Resources and Strategies

http://scratched.gse.harvard.edu/resources/debugging-scratch-resources-and-strategies

Includes links to forums, tutorials, and more resources for learning to debug.

Tynker: Debugger

https://www.tynker.com/hour-of-code/debugger

Practice solving problems with this debugging game.

What Is Debugging?

https://www.bbc.com/bitesize/articles/ztkx6sg

Describes types of bugs and how to think about removing them.

INDEX